RITUALS & CUSTOMS OF
A HINDU WEDDING

Design & Planning Guide

KAVITA KAPOOR

authorHOUSE®

AuthorHouse™ UK Ltd.
500 Avebury Boulevard
Central Milton Keynes, MK9 2BE
www.authorhouse.co.uk
Phone: 08001974150

First published by AuthorHouse 10/24/2007

ISBN: 978-1-4343-1927-2 (sc)

Printed in the United States of America
Bloomington, Indiana

This book is printed on acid-free paper.

ACKNOWLEDGEMENTS

The need for this book first became apparent when my nephew and niece got married. My elder sister, Santosh Paul asked me to write down details of the ceremonies as none of us knew what we had to do. The straw that broke the camel's back was when we experienced the panic and frustrations of our friends and relatives at another wedding. My brother, Ashvin Sunak then felt that this book was really needed and so I began the arduous task of putting this book together. It has been a labor of love for me to write this book. I would like to thank my brother Ashvin Sunak, my sister Santosh Paul, my brother in law Dr. Mahendar Paul for his support, encouragement and the photographs in this book. He also very kindly designed the cover of this book. There are a number of other people who have contributed greatly by giving me guidance, advice and positive suggestions when I was writing this book. They are my friend Dr. Mamta Misra, my son Dr. Karan Veer Kapoor, my colleague Mr. Tony Curwen and my husband, Krishan Kapoor. I would like to extend my very special thanks to all these people. I could not have reached the final stage without their help.

I hope that all who use this book find it helpful and that it gives them some exposure as to why we do what we do when performing a Hindu Wedding.

1

卐 ।। श्री गणेश शलोक: ।। 卐

वक्रतुंड महाकाय सूर्य कोटि समप्रभं ।।
निविध्नं कुरू मे देव सर्वकार्येषु सर्वदा ।।

vakratu.nDa mahaakaaya koTisuuryasamaprabha |
nirvighnaM kuru me deva sarvakaaryeshhu sarvadaa

PREFACE

Most Hindu Weddings follow a similar pattern. There are some regional variations, for example, the Hindus go around the fire while the Sikhs perform the wedding pheras around the Guru Granth Sahib in a Gurudwara. The Gujratis call the Sangeet Ceremony "Sangi" etc etc. These variations will be explained in detail in my future endeavors.

The planning process for weddings is common to all Indians and I hope this book will remove some of your panic moments and replace them with calm and serenity. When you are in control of the functions you are doing and know why you are doing them and how to do them, it makes it all easy to cope with things. The golden mantra is keep It simple, communicate with each other and delegate where possible. Relationships built on trust and understanding are priceless gifts, therefore, make sure you enjoy these priceless gifts.

I wish you all Happy Planning and a successfully accomplished Wedding Ceremony.

Contents

General Information

The Hindu Wedding is one of the liveliest and a very colorful occasion, with some ceremonies beginning months before the actual wedding day while other commence just weeks or a few days before the actual wedding day. The whole period of the wedding has an almost carnival-like atmosphere.

The ceremonies are listed in the order in which they take place and a table has been included to highlight the ceremonies which are mandatory and the ceremonies which are optional. The decision as to which of the optional ceremonies you want to hold could be made either individually or by joint discussion between the bride's and groom's families, the "two parties". Most of the ceremonies involve both parties and talking to each other during this process makes it easier for both families. Constant communications will ensure that both parties are aware of the ceremonies and what is expected of them when the ceremonies are being performed.

It is therefore, essential that you select and agree the ceremonies you are going to hold at home and the ceremonies which are going to be held at an external venue. Do not leave any ceremony undecided and hope for things to happen.

Another very important aspect of the planning process is that both parties should communicate effectively with each other and understand that, if one party has any special requirements, these are discussed, agreed and adhered to. It is not a good idea to keep things in your mind. If you do so, this will lead to disappointment and misunderstandings. Such issues can increase the tension between the two families when good relationships are just developing. One should not be afraid to raise matters of importance during the discussions, as this process will clear the air and lead to a happy and pleasant environment. This point is especially important for the bride's family as our culture expects the groom's family's needs to be accommodated.

Hindu Ceremonies Listing

Ceremonies to be performed before the Wedding day

Ceremony	Timing
1. The Civil Marriage	A couple of months/ weeks before the wedding day.
2. Sagan & Chunni Ceremony	Immediately after the Civil Marriage or a few days/weeks before the Hindu Wedding
3. Watna, Sangeet and Mehndi	A week or 3 to 4 days before the Wedding Day.
4. Gana & Chura Ceremony	2 to 3 days before the Wedding Day.

Ceremonies to be performed on the Wedding day prior to the Hindu Wedding

Ceremony	Timing
1. Groom Preparation	In the morning of the wedding day.
2. Bride Preparation	Take into account the arrival time of the Baraat.
3. Departure of the Baraat	Take into account the travel time and the arrival time of the Baraat
4. Reception of Baraat and Milni	At the venue of the Wedding
5. Dwar Puja	At the venue of the Wedding

The Hindu Wedding Ceremony Ritual Listing

1. Varmala

2. Madhu Parka

3. Shoe Grabbing

4. Kanyadaan

5. Ganth Bandhan

6. Mangal Fere

7. The Lajohom

8. Saptapadi

9. Shilarohan

10. Sehra Vadai

11. Doli/Vidai

Bride's Reception at the Groom's House

1. Pani Varna

2. Gana and Kangana Khalna

OPTIONAL CEREMONIES

Ceremony	*Timing*
1. Roka	A couple of months before the Wedding Day or as per convenience of the parties concerned.
2. Ghar Ghardol	3 – 4 days before the Wedding Day. This ceremony can be tagged along the Watna and Sangeet ceremony.
3. Mooh Dikhi	After the doli at the residence of the groom. This ceremony can be tagged along with the Gana and Kangana Khalna ceremony.
4. Puja of the Ancestors	Mid morning, the day after the arrival of the Doli at the Groom's residence.
5. Phera Dalna	As per the convenience of the bride and groom and their families.

Start the Planning Process

Initial Planning Tasks between the Two Parties

- Agree in general the kind of wedding you want to have. The main issues of discussion are:

  The approximate number of people who will be attending the wedding and various other ceremonies.

  The type of venues that will be acceptable to both parties.

  Will there will be sufficient parking facilities, both at home and at the venue being selected.

  What arrangements have been made for guests coming from overseas and longer distances both at home and at the venue?

  If hotel accommodation is required, what distances will the guests have to travel to reach the place of the ceremony?

  Give each other time and space to do private research.

  Do not rush with this debate. It is a crucial decision that will dictate all the planning process for the ceremonies.

- Select the main and optional ceremonies that you want to perform.

- Take a rough estimate of the numbers for each function.

- Another important discussion is the wedding reception which is held on the wedding day, after the Hindu wedding.

There are two options for the Wedding Reception:

> Both the bride's parents and the groom's parents hold their own wedding receptions.

> The parties hold a joint reception.

- Agree the date and month of the actual wedding and the alternative dates. Each party can then look at availability of venues and discuss the convenience of the dates with their family members.

- Take into account the weather conditions.

- Hold the ceremonies within a week or so of the wedding day so that family members', who have travelled from abroad, can partake in the ceremonies.

- Inform people of your initial plans at the earliest possible time so that everyone can start to plan their own commitments and avoid last minute panics.

- Remember that ceremonies held during weekdays might require some guests to take holidays from work. So plan these ceremonies in such a way that it causes the least inconvenience to the people attending the ceremony.

- Exchange all forms of communications - home addresses, telephone numbers, especially people who are going to help you in carrying out the ceremonies.

- Each party to have an overall budget estimate for their part of the wedding. This is important. Each party should know that they can cope with the financial pressure of the wedding.

- Make a list of the friends and family members who will be able to help in the planning and in the execution of ceremonies. You need a few dedicated family members to make a success of each ceremony.

- Have a voluntary workforce co-ordinator. This is an individual who will be responsible for organising this voluntary work force. The success of any wedding is in the use of the extended family members and friends in performing various tasks.

- Another very important point is that this involvement will make the wedding fun and more enjoyable for all. Giving people something to do gives them a feeling of being part of the festivities and it is excellent for motivation.

- Seating Plan is another very difficult task. If you have opted for named seating plan, give this job to a very amicable and approachable person. This will have to be changed a number of times before it is finalised.

- Make sure that there is reserved seating area for the bridal families. This is more important when you have open seating.

- Decide who is going to sit on the head table and how many family members will be giving speeches. Please keep these to a minimum. Short and sweet should be the aim.

Wedding Co-ordinators

- Now-a-days, wedding co-ordinators are available. If you wish to appoint a wedding co-ordinator, select the services that are being offered. The services they offer are:

- Total package – they provide all the decorations, items needed for the ceremony and someone to perform the ceremonies. Here the co-ordinators take full responsibility for everything and you are free to enjoy the wedding.

- They can deliver the items to you and you are responsible for the ceremony yourself. Agree delivery and pick up times, quantities etc. clearly and agree these in writing.

- You can select the items you want for your ceremony. You collect the items yourself and return them yourself.

- The price for each option will be different. So make sure you agree the price and the service details.

- If items are damaged, what are the charges? Check the quality of the items before hiring them or collecting them. Do not get charged for someone else mishandling.

It is also important to ask the wedding co-ordinator what additional services they provide and at what cost. These co-ordinators have good contacts with musicians, pandits etc. and can negotiate a complete package of services for you. Their rates are very competitive, but do compare their costs to what it will cost you when you go down the do it yourself route.

Detailed Planning Tasks for Each Ceremony

- Decide the venue and detailed timings for the function

- Agree the approximate numbers for the ceremony which is being planned.

- It is a very good idea to take notes and write things down. Use modern technology and use a computer so that you can send the information to each other after discussion for verification.

- Car parking, especially when the cars are big and occupy more space than smaller cars.

- Get the co-operation of the neighbours, especially when there will be congestion around the area, when ceremonies are held at home.

- Draw up your detailed guest list for each function.

- What is the seating plan e.g. by name or open for the various functions.

- Select the invitation cards and plan the words that have to be written.

- If you have separate cards for various ceremonies, ensure that you have listed all the ceremonies on the RSVP card.

- RSVP should specify the ceremony and the numbers attending that ceremony.

- Delegate the responsibility of sending out invitations and collating the RSVPs to a selected few individuals. Make sure that these individuals have got the correct names and addresses. No one likes an invitation with a wrongly spelled name or address.

- Nominate the person who will perform the ceremony – can a family member do this ceremony? If so, let this person know the time and place and what is expected from this individual. If not, then there is the need for a Hindu priest.

- Make sure that you have taken into account the needs and obligations of the other party.

- Book a professional photographer and/or DVD/Video maker.

- Hire your own professionals, as both parties have ceremonies of their own which they would like to capture.

- The bride and groom should plan their holidays, if they are hoping to go away after the wedding. The honeymoon is a very private affair. Speak to a travel agent/internet searching or otherwise and make your bookings accordingly.

Understanding the Ceremony and Tasks Involved

- Read about the ceremony and understand the purpose of the ceremony.

- Do not do any ceremony which you have not planned. Please adhere to timings.

- Think about who needs to be invited to the ceremony.

- Consider the venue you have selected for the ceremony. Are their any fire hazards that need to be taken into account? This is important when you are planning to do a Havan.

- Does the venue have additional requirements, for example, if the venue is external, do you need to have heaters or fans in the venue?

- Check you have all the ingredients for the ceremony that you are about to undertake. Verify the tick list on the box labelled with the ceremony.

- Is the voluntary workforce doing what is expected of them? Remember some people may need transport to and from the venue, so make sure this has been organised. The times of collection, taking into account the traffic conditions.

- If food is being served when the ceremony is concluded, have you thought through everything needed for preparation and serving?

- Book a pandit for the ceremony, if his presence is required. Discuss and agree his charges. Use your family members where possible to carry out simple ceremonies. Keep things simple and short.

- Choose a floral theme for a ceremony, if you so wish. Arrange with a florist and delegate this responsibility to someone in the family.

- If you are going to play music at the ceremony, get the appropriate CDs and a sound system at the venue. If you want to have live music, make sure you have booked a DJ and have told him the time of his arrival and departure and agreed the charges with him/her.

- What outfits are you going to wear? What outfits are the family members wearing? If you have selected a color scheme, then inform the relevant people of it.

- To ensure that all key family members look good, start this process early. Try out all outfits early, check that they fit well and think of all the accessories that have to go with the outfits, e.g. shoes, socks, sandals and any headgear etc.

- Keep check that your budget is not running wild.

- If you have made any changes, revisit the costs and make sure you have reflected these changes in the costs and increased or decreased the budget accordingly.

- If you have delegated responsibility to others for purchase of items, make sure you give them a list of things required and a budget limit – especially the upper limit.

CEREMONIES HELD AT HOME – DETAILED PLANNING TASKS

- If a ceremony is being held at home, make sure that you can accommodate all the guests at your residence.

- Think carefully about the ceremony, the areas you will need for your guests to sit while performing the ceremony and when eating.

- Will the ceremony be held inside the house or outside in the garden? If it is going to be held in both locations:

    - What is the time of the ceremony?

    - Do you need a marquee?

    - Do you need heaters/fans?

    - What time is the photographer expected?

    - What are the catering arrangements?

    - Have you hired enough table and chairs?

    - Have you got sufficient supply of cutlery, plates and spoons, both for serving and eating.

    - Have you got ample connections for electricity, heat and lighting?.

- If you will need a marquee for a function at home, what would be the size of the marquee? The marquee can provide good cover from the elements even if the weather is good. How are you going to decorate and provide electricity in the marquee. Make sure there are no trailing wires which can be a health hazard.

- Select the area where the marquee will be installed? Who will install it and dismantle it. Who will be responsible for decorating the marquee?

- Decide where you will cook the food, ie at home or you will get external caterers to provide cooked meals. Have you got facilities to re-heat the food? If not, then these will have to be hired. Can the caterers provide a total package of services for the ceremony including drinks? If so, consider these options.

- Will you need to hire waiters or waitresses for your home ceremony? What will it cost to hire them? Can the caterer provide waiters etc. and what will the cost of this service be.

- Caterers usually charge a rate per plate, so make sure you take into account the number of children, vegetarians and non-vegetarians when discussing catering costs.

- Will you need help around the house to keep things tidy and clean? If so, cost the services of a cleaner in the budget. Work out the number of hours you would need the cleaner for, how the cleaner will get to the house and what duties the person will be expected to perform.

Home Cooking

This is normally very difficult unless the total number of guests is between 30-40. To cook at home for larger numbers needs special gas cylinders and gas hobs with larger pots and pans. If you are going down this route:

1. Plan the menu carefully taking into account the number of vegetarian or non-vegetarian dishes.

2. Buy all ingredients in advance and try and prepare some items in advance e.g. onions, garlic, ginger etc. (where possible, use ready prepared supplies such as fried onions, ginger, garlic, chillies etc.).

3. Decide the time when the voluntary force will be arriving to help you with the cooking.

4. Where will the food be stored after cooking?

5. Who will be responsible for re-heating the food?

6. Who is the dedicated individuals responsible for the seating arrangements for the function?

7. Who is in charge of serving and refilling?

8. What is the time when the starters and the main course will be served?

9. Are you going to use disposable plates or china dishes? If you are using china, then you will need volunteers to help to clear these plates after each serving.

10. Serve smaller helpings to avoid wastage.

11. If you have opted for a buffet service, you still need an attendant so that young children can be helped with serving.

12. What drinks will be served? If liquor is being served, delegate this responsibility to a level headed person.

13. If you need to keep drinks cold, have you got storage space for this? How, when and where from will you get ice and ice buckets etc. Bags of ice are available at most petrol stations.

14. Make appropriate arrangements for serving hot drinks like tea and coffee. Use insulated cups for this purpose.

15. Are you, once again, using disposables or china? It is better to opt out for disposables, especially when you are performing ceremonies at home.

Ensure that you involve family members who are helpful and not a hindrance. Family members at weddings are more than willing to help but they need to be asked. SO ASK!! Give someone responsibility so that you are not doing it all on your own, especially when you want to serve drinks and dinner at your function. When you delegate a responsibility to another individual, it makes the other person feel valued and important and at the same time it gives you time to talk to your guests and enjoy the function.

SHOPPING LIST FOR HOME COOKING

Vegetables as per menu- quantity estimated no. of guests	
Lentils as per menu – quantity estimated no. of guests	
Oil frying	
Ginger, chillies,dhania, onions etc.	
Salt, pepper, garam masala etc. (usual Indian condiments)	
Non vegetarian items as per menu	
Utensils for cooking	
Gas and stoves for cooking	
Temporary area dedicated for cooking	
Helpers for preparing the vegetables	
Helpers for cooking the food	
Helpers for lifting heavy and big utensils	
Food storage area	
Hire - tables and chairs	
Table cloths, napkins, plates, glasses & spoons for serving and eating	
Milk, Tea, Coffee and sugar	
Tea/Coffee area and dispensers	
Purchase of both soft and hard drinks	
Hire chaffing dishes and fuel burners to keep the food hot	
Dedicated space for a temporary Bar	
Lighting of the various area	
Caterers - Full package excluding drinks (based on estimated numbers)	
Caterers – Delivery of cooked food	
Caterers – Serving of food with waiter service	
Own waiter service or voluntary workforce	
Marquee – lighting, heating and fans	
Food, drink and refreshments for the volunteer force during the preparation time.	
Car parking and neighbourhood considerations	
Clearing and disposal of rubbish	
Additional items Required:	

EXTERNAL CATERING

1. Agree with the caterer what he is providing. Make note of all the items that he supposed to provide, e.g. starters, main course and desserts – full detail of the menu. Have a trial run of the food that will be served.

2. If he is providing drinks, what soft drinks are included and if he is providing liquor, then what brands of liquor he is going to serve. Agree a maximum number of servings per person to keep track of the costs.

3. Decide the approximate number attending and have a margin of error of say 2% either way.

4. If you have agreed a cost per head, make sure you have a breakdown of what is the cost of the food, drinks and liquor. Make sure you have some way of verifying the costs, when you receive the bill.

5. The caterers are very accommodative and make allowances for different age groups that attend the wedding functions.

6. It is the responsibility of the caterers to ensure that there is sufficient food and drink.

7. Make sure you have discussed the number of waiters and waitresses you will need for the ceremony. Sometimes, too few waiters and waitresses can slow down the serving and cause distress to the guests.

8. Try all the dishes in the menu that you have selected. Verify the quality and the standard of the food that is going to be served. Take references from other people who have used these caterers before.

9. Agree the times when the caterers have to arrive at the venue. Take contact numbers, both land lines and mobiles so that you can ensure things go smoothly.

10. Check and make sure that there is a back-up in case of problems.

PLANNING LIST

Functions at a venue	
Functions at home	
Estimated no. of guests finalised with various parties	
Names and addresses of guests	
Invitations and acceptances co-ordinated	
Seating Plan	
Bride & Groom's party seating arrangements	
Times of starting and ending of ceremonies	
Neighbours	
Parking	
Health & Safety	
Journey times to various ceremonies	
Accommodation for guests arriving from overseas and long distances.	
Volunteer workforce	
The Pandit if required or a nominated family member	
Music CD and/or DJ	
Photographer	
Easy access to power points	

Names and contact numbers	
Hiring of utensils	
Purchases of food items	
Purchases of serving items	
External caterers	
Details of the package verified	
Mixture of self catering and external caterers	
Decorations for the home/venue	
Theme of the ceremony – flowers etc.	
Team of decorators – names and contact numbers	
Time planning for the assembly, removal and return of various items.	
Trial run of your outfits	
Verification of your travel plans	
Documentation for your travels	
Travel cases and clothes	
Additional Items:	

- The Roka ceremony has been done, if you had one.

- The family members have been informed, especially those travelling from abroad. They have all the information of the various wedding ceremonies.

- All wedding invitations have been sent out and acceptances are being received.

- All Pre-Wedding Ceremonies have been planned and bookings have been confirmed in writing.

- There is open communication between both parties and everyone is happy and that there are no unresolved issues.

- The shopping list has been ticked and items have been purchased.

- The contracts have been signed and accepted by the various parties concerned. For example, a pandit, external venues, marquees, caterers, florists, mandap, cars, photographer etc. for the various ceremonies.

- Start a follow up on wedding invitation guests who have not replied so far to check if they are attending and how many members will be present.

- List the number of adults and children who will be attending. This will be needed when you have to confirm the numbers with the caterers, or when you are cooking yourself.

- Label each box with the ceremony and paste the tick list on it. Put the non-perishables in the container. You will only have the perishable items outstanding.

- Maintain good contacts with all the people who have delegated responsibilities, especially the voluntary work force.

- Check the table seating plan for the guests, the reserved seating plan for the bride and groom's family.

- If the seating plan is open, check that there is a reserved seating area for the bride and groom's family.

- Plan the route of the journey from home to the wedding venue. If the distance is longer, check starting and returning times, refreshments on route and comfort breaks during the journey.

- Casual wear for the bride and groom during the journey.

- Allocation of changing rooms for the bride and groom.

- Choose engagement/wedding rings.

- Check with the suppliers the availability of the items that have been rented or hired. Agree with supplier the times of collection and return and the costs related to breakages etc.

- Plan your shopping trips in such a way that you do not have to make too many journeys. Check if on line ordering is possible. Sometimes you can get excellent deals by surfing the net.

- Shop for various gifts that you have to give to the relations. Try and keep these simple. Gifts are just a gesture of goodwill, so buy items which are a memento of the wedding.

- Book accommodation for out of town guests or provide them with information where they can stay and they can do their own booking.

- Fix a date for your Hen and Stag night parties.

- Plan the activities, transportation to and from the venue.

- The numbers who will be attending the party

- Allocate a budget for this party and make sure you keep a check of the expenditure, especially the booze.

- Plan your menu for the various functions. Self catering or external caterers. Agree the prices.

- Review the Wedding Day Preparation and begin the ground work.

- Make appointments with the hair dresser and beautician etc.

- Organise mehandi artist and extra artists who will do mehandi for the family members.

- Book appropriate means of transport for the groom's Baraat and Doli ceremonies.

- Refreshments and comfort breaks, subject to the distances being travelled.

- Finalise your holiday plans, take leave, make sure your passports and vaccinations are up to date and you have got all the necessary documentation.

- Travel cases and appropriate clothing for the holidays.

- Be sure your wedding clothes are collected, ironed and ready to wear.

- Verify the "Tick Lists "on each ceremony container to make sure that the missing items have been included, leaving only the perishables.

- All the gifts and presents have been wrapped and labelled. It becomes much easier to hand out labelled gifts and it avoids all confusions.

- Add up all that you have spent so far and make sure that you are on budget.

- A final recap between the two parties to make sure that both parties are happy with the arrangements and timings etc.

- Revisit and confirm the final plans for all the ceremonies that are going to be held at various venues.

- Finalise and review the table seating plan. Organise reserved seating arrangement for the Baraat party at the venue. Share the table plan with the bride and groom's family to prevent any wedding day misunderstandings.

- Make a personal visit to all external venues and key suppliers and check that all bookings and requirements are accurate and that everyone supplying goods or services understands what is expected of them. **Do not overlook this re-checking**. This is an important re-assurance step that things are going as per the plan.

- Finalise the numbers for various functions and inform the relevant parties of the change in numbers, if any.

- Buy the "Varmalas" in consultation with the bride and the groom. If the "Varmalas" are made of fresh flowers, then make sure the florist who is making them, knows of the colours and the lengths of the garlands.

- The wedding Mandap and the decoration of the wedding venue are finalised. If you have gone for a full wedding package service, check that the theme is as per your selection.

- If you are doing it yourself, check that the volunteer work force and the person who has been delegated to do this has all the necessary things.

- Make sure the delegated member visits the venue so that he/ she can assess what is needed. Sometimes, one can overlook a simple thing like a ladder which can make it very difficult to put up decorations.

- Book a Dhol player to lead the baraat party at the wedding venue and for the other functions. You can get a family member play the dhol for you if you have someone with this talent in your family.

- Re-confirm wedding car booking and/or coach booking, as appropriate for the baraat party.

- Re-confirm the booking with the photographer.

- If you are decorating the wedding car yourself, make sure your voluntary workforce arrives in time to get this done.

- Think about all the ceremonies that will need decorations and delegate this task to the younger members of the family (both boys and girls). This will make them feel part of the ceremony and is also a way of bonding the family. It makes the ceremonies much more fun and enjoyable.

Let's get cracking ...... 2 weeks to go!

- Inform relevant parties if there are any changes to the number of guests attending or any changes to any other ceremony.

- Check the detailed planning of each ceremony and be assured that everything will be ok.

- Arrange for all the clothes to be ironed and packed ready for the ceremonies.

- Arrange all the boxes and containers in the order of the ceremonies.

- If these boxes need to be transported, appoint a nominated individual who is responsible for transporting these boxes.

- Recap with telephones or emails that all arrangements with all the suppliers of goods and services are in order.

- Make final checks on all your bookings.

- Verify the holiday arrangements and order travellers cheques or appropriate currency, if needed.

- Speak to all the family members and friends who have been delegated tasks and check that everything is running smoothly.

- Verify arrangements with professionals, caterers etc.

- Try out the outfits and make sure that they do not need alterations.

- Just a gentle reminder to the volunteers that they are still willing and responsible for their activities.

- Pack your suitcase ready for your holidays

Relax.... The day before the wedding!

- Relax and take long luxury baths and showers.

- Listen to soft music and have plenty of cool drinks.

- Everything will be OK

PRE WEDDING CEREMONIES

Civil Marriage Ceremony

A civil marriage ceremony can take place in any register office in England or Wales, or at any venue that has been approved to hold a civil marriage. Approved premises include stately homes and other prestigious buildings, hotels and restaurants. Many Hindu temples are Approved premises and some priests are approved registrars.

The timing of this legal registry depends upon the wishes of the two parties. Many a families perform the Civil marriage prior to the commencement of the Hindu wedding. The couple are declared man and wife by the Civil marriage.

If the civil wedding is held a couple of months prior to the Hindu wedding, then the very close relations of both parties are invited to the ceremony.

In our culture, the couple are accepted as husband and wife when the Hindu Wedding Ceremony has been completed.

Civil Marriage information can be downloaded from www.gro.gov.uk/gro/content/marriages

Hindu Rituals

Sagan & Chunni Ceremony

The Sagan ceremony is an engagement ceremony of the groom. In the past this ceremony was considered the official engagement of the groom to the bride and the family of the bride with their family and friends came to the house of the groom to perform this ceremony. The Sagan ceremony is held before the Chunni ceremony.

The Chuni ceremony is the engagement of the bride. The ceremony is performed by the mother of the groom at the home of the bride.

The popular change to this ceremony is that both Sagan and Chuni are now-a-days performed at the residence of the groom, or a venue selected by them. This ceremony is sometimes performed after the civil marriage in order to keep the ceremonies to a minimum.

The Sagan Process

- The groom is seated on a decorated seat.

- The bride's family brings a sagan package to the house or venue selected by the groom's family and place it on a table allocated for it.

- The bride's father comes forward and puts a tilak (mark on the forehead using Kum kum, the red power, made into a paste using water) on the forehead of his future son-in-law.

- After the tilak, he then applies some uncooked rice to his forehead.

- He feeds his son-in-law with some methai from the sagan package.

- The son-in-law gets up and touches the feet of his father-in-law for his blessings.

The Chunni Process

The groom's mother, accompanied by her family and friends goes to the residence of the bride with a Chunni package. If this is a joint function, being held by the groom's family, then:

- The bride is invited to come and sit next to the groom, for the Chuni ceremony.

(The clothes, the bride wears for this ceremony are given to her by the groom's family. In order to make things easy for the bride, these clothes are given to her in advance so that she can get ready without any inconvenience).

- The bride is seated next to the groom.

- The groom's mother comes forward with the chunni package.

- She takes a chunni (scarf) and drapes the Chunni around the shoulders of the bride.

- She then puts red and gold bangles in both the hands of her daughter-in-law.

- She gives her daughter-in-law some dried fruit, and some methai to eat which she has brought in the Chunni package.

- She blesses the bride by placing her hand on her head, better still giving her a hug, making sure that she does not ruin her daughter-in-law's hairstyle.

- *The bride and the groom exchange rings if they have not had a civil wedding before this ceremony.*

- The family members then come forward and bless both the bride and the groom. This blessing is a gentle hug. Each family member gives the bride some gift to welcome her in their family. To keep things simple, this gift is generally money.

THINGS NEEDED FOR THE CEREMONIES ARE:

Sagan.	
1 Thali	
1 pkt of kum kum – red powder	
Handful of uncooked rice	
1 small bowl to mix kum kum with water.	
1 engagement ring	
Sagan package made up of methai, dried fruit, etc.	
Chunni	
Complete set of clothing for the bride	
A chunni - scarf	
Some red and gold bangles	
1 pkt of henna	
India sweets	
1 engagement ring	
Chunni Package, made up of dried fruit, methai etc.	

The above is a basic minimum but a sagan and chuni package can be as elaborate as the families like it to be. Many a families prefer to keep things to a minimum and make life easy.

All the members of the respective families congratulate each other and the ceremony is concluded. The bride and groom's respective families share the ingredients of the sagan and the chunni package with their relatives.

The ceremony is concluded with dinner and dancing.

WATNA, SANGEET & MEHNDI

The above ceremonies start the festivity and frolic that leads up the wedding day. It is a statement that both the bride and the groom are accepting the changes life is going to bring forth. It also marks the start of the arrival of guests from both near and far for the wedding.

Watna is a pack made out of herbal ingredients, which is applied to make the bride and the groom look beautiful on their wedding day.

Sangeet is the singing of traditional wedding hymns and songs. This session brings families together, and it is a time when family members get an opportunity to tease each other and have fun. The singing is normally on one night but it can carry on for a couple of nights if there are family members who have come from far to attend the wedding and want to enjoy the occasion to the maximum. The family members use a traditional "dholki" (a percussion drum) as an accompaniment for the singing.

Mehndi is putting of henna on the hands of both the bride and the groom. By putting mehndi (henna), the family and friends are wishing that the union seeks green pastures, the colour of the henna when dry, and their life be rosy, the colour henna leaves behind when it is washed off.

According to Hindu scriptures, every one of us goes through four stages of life:

"Bramcharya" – unmarried - the time of life when you are growing up i.e. childhood and early adulthood. In this period an individual is supposed to learn – time of life to get educated.

"Grahast" – Adulthood – the time of life when one is going to take on the responsibilities of a householder.

"Sanyas" - Learning of scriptures – the time of life when you are older and in this period you hand over the responsibilities to the younger generation and spend more of your time learning the scripture, salvation and spirituality.

"Vanparst" – Disperse the information – the time of life when the knowledge is imparted to others, time when one sometimes leave one's home to do service for the community and help others who are not that fortunate in life.

The vows listed above prepare both the bride and the groom for "Grahast" and the parents for letting go of things so that they can eventually move towards "Sanyas". These activities gears both generations for the changes that are going to confront them in the near future.

Groom
As a general rule "Watna, Sangeet and Mehndi" the three ceremonies are held on the same day for the groom, i.e. the Watna ceremony is performed early evening, followed by sangeet. The mehndi ceremony is done during the singing session.

Bride
For the bride the family prefer to do Watna a day before the Sangeet and mehndi ceremony. The reason is that it takes a bride much longer to get dressed up and if the watna ceremony does get out of hand, the bride gets enough time to wash off the watna and sort herself out. The watna ceremony for both the bride and the groom is a close-knit family affair.

There is no fixed time for the above ceremonies and the time is arranged in consultation with the family members who are going to take part in the ceremony.

The Process - Watna for the Bride and the Groom

- A small stool or a low seat is placed in the middle of the room.

- A red chunni is held like a palanquin over the seat.

- The bride/groom is asked to come and sit on the seat.

- The bride/groom's mother takes the watna (paste made with wheat flour, turmeric and oil) and rubs this on the face, arms and legs of the bride/groom. All the family members and friends take turns to do the same.

- The bride/groom is allowed to take revenge and apply watna on the faces of those who take an undue advantage of their patience.

- Most of the times, the watna sessions ends up with more than the bride/groom covered in the watna paste.

- Make sure you have taken precautions to keep the décor in order.

- When everyone has had there go, then the bride/groom is fed with some methai (Indian sweet) and they move from the seat.

- All those who are covered in watna get the opportunity to wash themselves and sort themselves out.

- The bride/groom takes a bath and get ready for the next ceremony.

The ceremony is concluded by the mother of the bride/groom, stepping over the seat, where the bride/groom had been sitting. She does this five times. She does not put her foot on the seat, and that is why a low seat is preferred. She does this to ward off any evil eye and bad omens. The seat is then removed.

Food, drink and refreshments are optional extras.

Sangeet:

The family members get together and start the singing session, by starting with songs which are traditional i.e. 'ghori' songs for the groom and 'suhaag' songs for the bride. Sometimes the professional drum (dhol) players or bhangra DJs are invited to make the ceremony more enjoyable. Others just invite professional singers for the singing session, but generally, the family members chip in and make sangeet an informal fun time. The ceremony is concluded with dinner and dancing.

The Mehndi Ceremony

The singing is stopped for a short while and the mehndi ceremony is carried out for the groom. For the bride it is a much longer session.

The Groom

- The groom is given a comfortable seat to sit on.

- The groom's mother puts some henna on her son's right hand.

- She just puts the sign of OM on her son's right hand.

- In the modern times, the groom, now-a-days asks the professional henna painters to put his bride's name on his hand.

- This is a fairly quick session for the groom and he can then join in the singing and dancing.

- The female members' of the family and friends then get the professional henna painter to put mehndi on their hands. This goes on in parallel to the singing session.

- Some females like to have fun and they paint each others hands.

THE BRIDE

- The bride is given a more comfortable seat for the mehndi, as her session takes much longer.

- The bride's mother gives the professional artist the mehndi that was in the chunni package and the professional artist starts to put the henna pattern on the bride.

- The female members of family and friends also get their hands painted. It is up the family to have extra henna painters for the family.

- The occasion is graced with singing and dancing. If Sangeet is on the same day, then the bride needs space of her own to get her mehndi done.

- Many families prefer to have the bride's henna ceremony to be a close knit family affair and they have Sangeet on another day.

Things needed for the ceremony are:

Watna	
A red chunni	
A small stool or any other low seat	
A bowl of wheat flour	
Spoonful of turmeric power	
Oil – almond or other as per preference	
Some methai	

Sangeet	
A dhoki Indian folk dance percussion instrument (can be hired)	
A Professional Drum Player or a DJ or both.	
Drinks, refreshments and dinner as per the family's preference.	

Mehndi	
Extra mehndi tubes	
Henna painters (*agree the rates with the painters for the bride and the guests*).	
Drinks, refreshments and dinner are optional extras.	

The concluding activity is serving of refreshments and giving the attendees a gift of Indian methai as they leave. It is not necessary to give Indian methai, you can give whatever you think best. This gift is a token gesture to thank the attendees.

Gana & Chura Ceremonies

The gana is tied to both the bride and the groom. The chura ceremony is only for the bride.

Now-a-days this ceremony is held at the home of the Mamas (bride's mother's brothers). Alternative choices are the bride's parental home or a venue selected by them. These are welcome changes, which take a bit of the pressure off the bride's parents.

These two ceremonies are a reminder that the bride's brothers and cousin brothers' who, when they gave their sister away had promised to stand by her. When they do this ceremony they are now fulfilling that promise to their sister. This is a difficult time for the bride's mother, who now has to prepare herself to give away her daughter in marriage. The brothers give their sister moral support and make her accept that her daughter has to move on in life. This ceremony reinforces the bond between brothers' and sisters'.

The **Gana** ceremony is tying a string made up of five different metals on the right hand wrist of the bride and groom. It is believed that this string protects the bride/groom from evil influences. It is a representation of the five natural elements. The Gana is available at most wedding shops.

The Chura

The **Chura** is putting red bangles in the hands of the bride. The Gana and the Chura is removed when the bride reaches the house of the groom after their wedding. Most brides keep the Chura on for a couple of months prior to removal, but the Gana is removed when the Doli reaches the groom's house. In the olden times the brides' kept the Chura for a year and removed it on their first wedding anniversary but things and times have changed now. The removal of the Chura is a very personal thing. There are no hard and fast rules as to when the chura is removed.

GANA & CHURA CEREMONY – BRIDE

- The Chura ceremony is for the bride only.

- The maternal uncle of the bride (mama) and maternal aunt (mami), take a lead in performing this ceremony.

- The Mamas and the Mamis (maternal uncle and aunt) buy the chura (red bangles and 2 iron bangles) for the bride-to-be.

- This is normally done in consultation with the bride to ensure that the chura matches the wedding outfit.

- The Kileray (silver and gold umbrella shaped dangling ornaments) are purchased by family members and friends. These are tied to the iron bangles as part of the chura.

- Mostly the mamas' and mamis' buy the kileray with the chura, in consultation with the bride and give these to other members of the family.

- Now days the brides prefer to put only one "kilery" on each hand, so the members of the family just touch the kilery and give their blessings.

- The mamas can decide among themselves who is going to do the honours.

ACTIVITIES OF THE CHURA CEREMONY

a. The bride is asked to come and sit under a palanquin cover seat. She is given a red chunni to cover her head and the eldest mama takes the Gana and ties it on the right hand of the bride. (If there are more than one mamas' they all touch the Gana and give their blessings).

b. The mamas' and mamis' take a large bowl and put some water and milk (kachi lasi) into it (milk and water is in equal proportions).

c. The red bangles, the chura is put in the bowl of kachi lasi. (not the iron bangles). *Make sure that the Chura is kept tied with thread, so that the bangles for the right and left hand do not get mixed up. This is important as the bangles of the chura are in ascending order, so you start putting the largest bangles first and the smallest at the end.*

d. The mamas and mamis pick up the bowl with the chura, the iron bangles and sit around the bride.

e. The eldest mama and mami take a few bangles from the right hand pack of the chura from the bowl of kachi lasi.

f. The mami holds the bangles and the mama starts putting the bangles on the bride, starting with the largest bangles going first.

g. The bangles are in ascending order. The last bangle is the iron bangle.

h. The same procedure is followed for the left hand. (If there are more than one mamas' and mamis', then each one of them can take turns to put a few bangles in the hands of the bride).

i. After putting the chura in both hands, the mamas and mamis then tie "kileray" to the bride.

j. The family members tie kileray as well. If she has not opted out for just one kilery each.

k. The mamas and the mamis bless the bride and feed her some sweets.

l. The bride's mother then gives the mamas' and mamis' some gifts. Here she is thanking her brothers and sister-in-laws for doing the ceremony.

m. In order to conclude the ceremony, the mamas and mamis then give the bride and her family gifts in return. This is called "Nanky Chak". This is a gift by the maternal family to their sister and brother-in-law. A lot of teasing goes on at this time because the maternal relations and the paternal relations are showing off to each other. The "Nanky Chak" is becoming less important as the couple have wedding lists and families pick gifts from these lists. All other family members, if they wish can give their gifts at this time.

n. The brothers of the bride come forward and take her from the palanquin seat.

o. The bride does not have to keep the kileray on all the time. These are bulky and it is therefore an acceptable custom for the bride to remove the kileray and put them on just before she is leaving for the wedding mandap on the wedding day.

GANA CEREMONY – GROOM

The gana is tied to the groom as well.

- The process **a, k, l, and m** are common to both.

Things required for this ceremony are:

Red palanquin cover	
Chura (red bangles)	
2 Iron bangles	
A bowl	
Kileray	
Gana	
Water & Milk (Kachi Lasi)	
Indian sweets	
1 low sitting stool or pufay	
Gifts for the mamas and mamis by the bride and groom's mother	
Other gifts by the paternal and maternal relations for the bride and groom.	

The ceremony comes to a closure when the family members hug each other and rejoice. Refreshments are served to conclude the ceremony.

WEDDING DAY
RITUALS

Wedding Day - Groom Preparation

The ceremonies are held on the wedding day, prior to the groom getting ready for the wedding procession – the baraat. These ceremonies are:

- Take responsibility to provide for the family – breaking 4 earthen pots

- Acceptance of changes that life will bring – Sehrabandi

- To look after the honour of the family – Pagri

The groom's attire is either traditional or western. The whole attire is:

> Pagri, (the headgear)
> Sehra (a dangling garland for the face)
> Mukat (a crown)

Sehrabandhi

Most families have their elders perform this ceremony. Others can call upon the services of a professional pandit, if you so wish.

The Process

- Put the whole attire in front of Lord Ganesh

- Say a small simple prayer to Lord Ganesh

- Take some Kesar (Saffron mixed with water and rice)

- Sprinkle this lightly over the groom's clothes (it is better to sprinkle on the inside so that the attire is not ruined)

- This attire is then handed over the groom.

- The pagri, sehra and mukut are left in front of Lord Ganesha for the sehra bandhi ceremony.

Breaking the earthen pots

After having taken a bath, the groom comes out of the bathroom. As he comes out, he steps over and breaks the four small earthen pots. These four earthen pots are placed on the ground face down. These pots represent the four new facets of life that he is about to embark upon, namely,

Dharm
Arth
Kam and
Moksh

(Detailed explanation of each of these words is on page 64).

The groom takes a vow that he will fulfil the duties of Dharam, Arth, Kam and Moksh. The broken pots are then disposed off. He wears the wedding attire.

The Process

- The groom is sat in front of Lord Ganesh and all members of the family and friends bless his sehra, mukat and pagri by touching it.

- The mother put the pagri on the forehead of her son, followed by the mukat and sehra.

- The family members sing blessings and the mother does the first varna and the other family members follow suite. (Varna is a blessing with some monetary value to ward off evil eye.

- The cash, which is collected, is then given to a charity of your choice.

Pagris for the Family members – Additional pagris (headgear) are given to the immediate male members of the family – the father, brothers, brothers-in-law, uncles, both paternal and maternal and friends if you so wish.

The parents of the groom give the pagri to the members of the family and they wear the headgear prior to joining the wedding procession. This is a form of identification of the immediate family members and useful when performing the milni ceremony.

SARBALA – THE BEST MAN

The sarbala is generally a young cousin in the family. He sits next to the groom at the time of sehrabandhi and he is also given a mukat and pagri just like the groom.

Nowadays this is not followed very strictly as grooms prefer to have a best man to help them around.

When everyone is ready, the groom leads the baraat, (the wedding party) outside of the house to where the cars of the baraat are parked.

The groom stands near the "Ghori" main car which is going to leading the baraat party. The last ceremony before the groom can sit in the vehicle is done by the sisters.

VAG FARAI

The sisters then do Vag Goodti (Vag Farai). Here the sisters bless their brother. The sisters and sisters-in-law tie a thread of mauli to the means of transport he is going to use. If it's a car, then they tie the mauli to the bonnet of the car. They want their brother to go safely and bring back his bride home safely.

The Dhol Players starts playing the dhol. He leads the Groom to the vehicle that is going to be the lead car for the barat party. The rest of the family follow him. The groom sits in the car with his sarbala. The family members embark in their transport.

(The ceremony is postponed if there is travelling involved. The ceremony is performed at the place where the baraat party is stationed prior to commencement of the wedding. This ritual is adapted accordingly).

THE DEPARTURE OF THE BARAAT PARTY

The baraat party is now ready to leave. The groom mounts the mare, or sits in the car or whatever means of transport he is using. The guests of the baraat party sit in their cars or whatever alternative transport is being used by the baraat party and head towards the wedding venue. The groom's car takes the top position and leads the baraat procession.

If the baraat is travelling a long distance, the groom can take off the sehra while he is travelling and put it on again when he has reached the venue. Sometimes, the groom prefers to wear a comfortable travelling gear and takes the blessed clothes with him and changes into them when he gets to the venue. These are adjustments that need to be made to accommodate the time and place of the wedding.

The same applies to the other members of the baraat party. This is especially so for the females who do not want to get their clothes creased up. Sometimes, the bride's and groom's family book changing rooms at the wedding venue. This just adds to the comfort and convenience of the guests accompanying the baraat party.

THINGS REQUIRED FOR THE CEREMONY ARE:

The groom's attire	
The sarbala's attire	
1 additional chunni for Gath Bandhan (to tie the knot at the time of pheras)	
1 Mangal Sutra	
1 Box of Sindhoor	
Garlands for Milni – number of garland depends upon the milnis planned.	
Pagris – again, depends up the number of close relations	
Cash money for varna	
Gifts for Vag Farai	
Change of clothes for the Bride on Doli – optional (to be discussed and agreed with the bride and her family)	
A Mare or car for Baraat	
A dhol player to lead the Baraat procession	
A coach or other transport arrangements if the marriage party is travelling a distance	
Refreshments when the baraat party is on route if required	
Wedding outfit of the groom if he travelling in casual clothes	

WEDDING DAY - BRIDE PREPARATION

There are no religious ceremonies that need to be performed by the bride when she is getting ready for the wedding day.

The bride takes her time and prepares for the most important day of her life by,

Visiting the hairdresser and the beauty parlour and pampering herself.

(Remember the shoes are taken off when you enter the mandap, so adjust the length of your costume to accommodate both with/without shoes.

Add any accessories as you wish e.g. handbags etc)

The bride usually wears a garment of her choice and the ritual colour is different shades of red. She can wear a sari, a langa (long skirt and blouse with a Chuni). This is her personal preference. The jewellery again is personal preference to match the costume.

Wedding Day - Baraat Reception

The bridal party have to be at the venue prior to the arrival of the baraat party, in order to greet the baraat party. The family members of the bride are normally eagerly awaiting the arrival of the baraat. The baraat arrives at the venue with much pump, show and dancing, and with a dhol player exciting the baraatis to do bhagra as they approach the wedding venue.

It is important for the groom's party to plan the route from the entrance of the venue to where the bride's party are waiting to receive them. It is always better to use stairs so that the total party can walk together. If lifts are being used, make sure that space is available for gathering at the start and end point before leading the baraat to the reception point.

The groom's baraat party arrive at the entrance of the wedding venue with the sound of Dhol (traditional Indian drum) and the family members performing the traditional bangra. The members of the bride's family and friends receive the groom's party as they approach the entrance. The baraatis await the official welcome, which is performed by a professional pandit who is going to perform all the rituals from here on, leading to the wedding ceremony.

The professional pujari (punditji) recites the mantras and welcomes the Baraat party. He calls upon the bride's family to start the milni ceremony.

One family member of the bride & groom is responsible for making sure that there are sufficient garlands. There is nothing worse than when the garlands have been left behind in excitement or they are in short supply.

Wedding Day - Milni Ceremony

The word "Milni" means meeting. Therefore, here the bride's family are coming forward to meet the groom's family and it is a kind of introduction. At the planning stage, the bride and groom's family have to decide the numbers and names of family members who are going to perform milni.

It is very important to agree the number of milnis that will be performed. The names of the relatives performing milni should be known to the bride's family in advance. The panditji calls out the name of each relation and they come forward to perform the milni ceremony. The milni is held between the immediate family members i.e. grandparents, father and mother, maternal and paternal relations, chacha and chachi, mama and mami, masi and masa, brother and sister in law and sister and brother in law.

Relations of the bride and groom, come forward, starting with the father of the bride and the groom.

- They walk forward and the bride's father garlands the groom's father. They give each other a hug and the bride's father gives a gift to the groom's father.

This activity is repeated for all other relations.

The exchange of gifts is optional. Many families prefer to exchange just garlands and no gifts. The exchange of gifts was done so that the groom's family would look favourably upon the bride. These days the bride and groom are equal partners in a marriage and the need for gifts has become less important. If you are exchanging gifts, then make sure that the gifts are parked next to the person responsible for the garlands on the bride's side. He/ she can hand out the garlands and the gift box as the family members come forward to greet each other.

THINGS REQUIRED FOR MILNI CEREMONY AND GUIDANCE ☑

A professional pandit.	
Garlands	
Gifts	

The professional pandit announces the end of the milni ceremony and asks the brothers of the bride to get the groom from the "ghori" or the car where he is sitting.

If the groom is accompanied the baraat party, due to constraints of the wedding venue, he stands at the back when the milni ceremony is being performed. The bride's brothers lead him to the front and the baraat party is asked to enter the wedding hall.

The bride's mother comes forward to do the next ceremony called the "Dwar Puja".

Dwar Puja

In this ceremony the mother of the bride welcomes the groom for the wedding ceremony. Dwar means a gate and puja is welcoming the groom

- The pandit recites the mantras

- The bride's mother puts a tilak on the groom's forehead using kum kum (red powder).

- She lights the diya.

- By rotating the thali round she performs aarti of the groom.

- She sprinkles flower petals on the groom and then on the floor where he is standing and sprinkles the water from the little kalas (circular metal pot).

- He is invited to enter the venue.

- The baraat party line up behind the groom in pairs, the unmarried brothers and sister on either side of the groom, and he leads them all to the wedding area, the Mandap*.

- He stands outside the Mandap, the four pillar canopy, and awaits the arrival of his bride.

- The baraat party is asked to take their reserved seats.

- The Hindu Wedding area is called a "Mandap" The four pillars canopy is placed in a prime position.

THINGS REQUIRED FOR DWAR PUJA CEREMONY ARE:

A plate	
Jyot	
Kalas filled with some water	
Kum Kum	
Match box	
Some flowers petal	
Some Ghee (clarified butter)	
A jyot holder	

The Bridal Entry

When everyone is seated, the bride walks in escorted by her sisters and cousin sisters. Her entry is full of grandeur with music and flower petals are thrown on the floor as she walks towards the mandap. She reaches the mandap and stands opposite the groom in front of the mandap

There has been a change here too. Now a days, the bride is escorted by her father rather than her sisters and the cousins. The sisters and cousins form part of the procession and throw flower petals as she is walking towards the mandap.

Varmala

Varmala – var means my beloved and mala means a garland, a garland for my beloved.

The garlands are handed to both the bride and the groom by the bride's family. The bride steps forward and garlands the groom. Then the groom welcomes his bride by garlanding her. All the guests present at the wedding indulge is much teasing and festivity to mark the happy union. Often, this ceremony acts as an effective icebreaker for the nervous bride and the groom.

The professional pandit asks the groom to walk into the mandap and take a seat followed by the bride. The parents of the groom are then escorted into the mandap by the bride's parents and seated. The bride's parents then take a seat in the mandap. As soon as the groom takes his shoe off, they are whisked away, why I will tell you later.

Madhu Parka

Madhu parka is a mixture of honey and yoghurt. Honey symbolises the sweetness in life and yoghurt the strength. This is offered by the bride to the groom who will eat the mixture three times. They promise to support each other in life.

Fun and Frolics for the Bride & Groom's families

Shoe Grabbing

This is really a fun part of the wedding. The groom and the bride have to take their shoes off when they enter the mandap. The shoes the groom is wearing are grabbed by the bride's sisters and cousins, supported by other members of the family and hidden away. The aim is that the groom's best man, the sarbala, will have to negotiate a price to get the groom's shoes back before the wedding ceremony has been completed.

This ceremony is full of fun and it is quite interesting to see the negotiations that go on between the bride's relations and the groom's sarbala, accompanied by his brothers and cousins. It is female power versus male power. The price can be anything, the best man and his team can be asked to do anything, within reason, by the female clan. They normally come to an agreement and return the shoes for a fee. This fee is shared by the bride's sisters and cousins. In the olden times, the fee was a ring made of gold or silver called "kalecharis". It was a remembrance of the wedding day shoe grabbing ceremony. Now-a-days some play acting and money seems to be the medium.

While these negotiations are going on, the panditji is carrying out his duties of performing the Hindu Wedding ceremony.

The Hindu Wedding Ceremony

The Puja

The pundit first performs puja for the groom. This puja is for the nine most important planets in the universe. The groom is asked to pray to them and ask them to bestow their blessing upon him and his bride. The groom chants the mantras after the pundit and follows the instructions given to him by the pandit as he chants the mantras.

The Hindu Marriage Ceremony is a religious occasion, the traditions and customs of which were created more than 35 centuries ago. The ceremony is performed in Sanskrit, the most ancient surviving language and root of all Indian dialects. The ceremony takes place in the Mandap. The sacred fire in the mandap not only symbolizes the illumination of the mind, knowledge and happiness, but also a clean and pure witness to the ceremony in progress.

The priest chants the "mantras" from the Vedas, the holy scriptures of the Hindus. The Havan Samgri – mixture of pure herbs and ghee are offered to the fire. The samgri purifies the atmosphere around us. He also offers fresh flowers to signify beauty, coconut to signify fertility, rice, and jaggy and other grains to signify food etc.: these are necessary ingredients to sustain life. Ghee (clarified butter) for the sacred fire, Kumkum (red powder used to signify good-luck).

The parents also partake in the puja. On completion of the havan, the panditji asks the bride and the groom to stand up for the holy reunion. He also asks the brothers of the bride to come to the mandap for the "Mangal Fere" (going around the holy fire).

Kanyadaan

The bride's parents put the hand of their daughter into the hands of the groom. He graciously accepts her by holding her hand.

GRANTH BANDHAN

The two ends of the scarves around the shoulders of the bride and groom are tied in a knot by the groom's mother. The knot is a symbol of unbreakable tie between the couple. They both stand up for the Mangal Fere.

The couple recite the verses after the priest. They stand up and are ready to take the four sacred vows.

MANGAL FERE- BACKGROUND

The couple circle around the sacred fire four times. The bride leads the first three and the groom leads the last one. With each phara, (the circle around the sacred fire) they seek the four basic goals of human life:

1. Dharm – religion, a sense to lead a good life

2. Arth – prosperity, to make life as happy as possible

3. Kam – to have energy and passion in life for their children

4. Moksh – detachment from worldly things and the attainment of the state of completeness with passing time.

The bride's brothers are called upon to the mandap. They all stand around the mandap in order to assist their sister when she is going around the sacred fire. The bride and the groom stand up to perform the first ceremony of the Mangal Fere, the Lajahom.

THE LAJAHOM

"Laja" is puffed rice, a symbol of prosperity.

- The groom extends both his hands forward and the bride puts her hands on top the groom's hands.

- The brothers put puffed rice in the cupped hands of their sister.

- Together, the bride and groom, offer this "laja" to the sacred fire.

- The bride leads the first phara with the brothers lending a helping hand to their sister.

- The above is repeated three times.

- On the fourth phara the groom is asked to lead the phera – saying that he will need her guidance and support in life and he will look after her.

SAPTAPADI (SEVEN VOWS)

The bride is led by the groom to take seven steps to symbolize the beginning of their journey through life together. These steps represent seven principles and the promises they make to each other.

1 *Together we shall cherish each other in sickness and in health, in happiness and in sorrow*

2 *Together we shall be lifelong friends*

3 *Together we shall share each other's ideals*

4 *Together we shall nourish each other's strengths, powers and fortune*

5 *Together we shall make each other happy*

6 *Together we shall love, provide and care for our children*

7 *Together we will look forward to the mysteries of the future with awe, open-mindedness and inspiration.*

On completion of the seven vows, the brothers lead their sister to perform Shilarohan.

SHILAROHAN

- The brothers of the bride place her right foot on a stone, while the priest recites the mantras.

- They express the wish that the marriage be as firm and as steady as the rock.

- The brothers promise that they will be there for their sister at all times.

- They then ask their sister to lift her foot off the rock.

- The brothers then leave the mandap.

The groom now makes the final promises to the bride. He promises to look after her and protect her by putting a "Mangalsutra" (a sacred Necklace traditionally made of black beads) on her, and then he puts sindoor (red powder) in the parting on the crown of the bride's head.

These two offerings signify the mark of a married woman and act as a symbol of the husband's love, integrity and devotion towards his wife. The bride now accepts the promises her husband has made and moves from the right side, where she has been sitting so far, to the left seat vacated by her husband.

Seven married women come forward and bestow their blessings on the bride by putting a ting of the "sindoor" in the bride's forehead.

The bride and the groom then get up and touch the feet of the groom's parents and their grandparents for blessing. Then the rest of the family come up to bless the couple. All the attendees sprinkle flower petals on newly wedded couple.

SHERA VADHAI (REMOVAL OF THE GROOM'S SHERA)

The bride's mother feeds her son-in-law and daughter with Indian sweets and then takes off the shera (the head gear) that the groom is wearing. This is then returned to the groom's mother at a later date.

RETURN OF THE SHOES

Hopefully by this time the negotiations have reached an amicable agreement and the groom can come down from the mandap and put on his shoes. If the agreement has not been reached, the poor groom has to walk bare foot, or assist in the negotiation process.

The ceremony is concluded when all the attendees congratulate the newly wedded couple. This is followed by a wedding reception where there is food, drink and dancing.

The things required for the Wedding Ceremony are:

Bride's Party

2 Garlands – Varmala – these are provided by the bride's family	
A havan kund (vessel in which the sacred fire is lit for puja)	
Samidha – wood for the havan	
Ghee – clarified butter	
Havan Samagi (ingredients for the havan)	
Dhoop (incense sticks)	
Pieces of karpoor (camphor)	
roli (a mixture of turmeric and lime)	
1 roll of mauli (red sacred thread)	
Matches	
6 bowls for havan	
Charan amrit – a bowl with the mixture of ghee, honey, ganga jal. Dhai (yoghurt) and milk	
4 thalis – 6" diameter for various puja ceremonies	
Water – in a kalas – Indian metal pot	
Honey and Yoghurt mixture Madhu Parka	
Some uncooked rice	
Raw supari (whole raw beetle nuts)	
Some Indian sweets	
Flower petals	
A small stone	
Puffed rice	

Groom's Party:

Sindhoor	
Mangal Sutra	
Money or other gifts for sisters, cousins and sister-in-law (Shoe Grabbing)	
1 spare chunni/scarf for Gath bandhan	
Change of Clothes for the Bride (optional)	

Doli or Vidai

The vidai ceremony is traditionally and usually performed at the residence of the bride. The bride is leaving her parental home – is the significance of this ceremony. This tradition is also changing and sometimes, the groom takes his bride home from the venue of the wedding. The very close family members follow the Doli procession as it leaves. The other guests bid their farewells to both parties after having, hopefully, enjoyed the reception.

This Doli ceremony marks the departure of the bride from her parental house. It is customary in some families to give the bride a change of clothes. The change of clothes is given to the bride, prior to the start of the wedding ceremonies by the groom's mother. The style and colour of the costume is pre-decided between the bride and her mother-in-law. Many a brides do not change their bridal costume prior to the Doli ceremony. If the Doli has to travel a long distance then the bride usually does change her bridal costume.

The timing of the doli ceremony is dependent upon the venue and the convenience of both families. Sometimes families bid farewell to the newly weds from the wedding hall as this is convenient and everyone present can give the newly weds a hearty send off.

THE PROCESS

- The bride and the groom are seated together.

- Each member of the family blesses them, one by one, starting with the parents of the bride.

- Both the bride and the groom stand up and the mother of the bride gives her daughter some phulian (puffed rice) in her cupped hands.

- She throws the phulian over her head. (If there are no phulian available, this ceremony can be done using uncooked rice and flowers).

- She conveys her good wishes for her parents through this gesture.

- She throws the phulian over her head five times and the brothers in the family catch some of these phulian as a promise that they will always stand by their sister.

- The groom then leads his bride to the car waiting to take them to the groom's house.

In the olden times it was customary for one of the brothers to accompany his sister when she left her parental home. This was just to give his sister moral support because she was not known to the in-laws. This is not the case in present times and the couple are well known to each other before they decide to get married.

The bride's family and friends throw flowers over the car before the procession leaves the venue and the doli starts its journey to the groom's house.

If the wedding party have travelled a long distance, then the doli heads towards the place where the baraat party is staying. The ceremonies that follow can be done where the baraat is staying or they can be postponed until the doli reaches the home and the ceremonies can be done then. There are, again no hard and fast rules for these ceremonies and they are accommodated taking into account the time and place of the wedding ceremony.

THINGS REQUIRED FOR THIS CEREMONY ARE:

Some puffed rice, or uncooked rice and flowers	
Some Indian sweets	
The car for the Doli	
Flower petals	
Change of clothes	

The Reception of The Bride into The Groom's House

Pani Varna

All the ceremonies at the Groom's house are a close knit family affair and only close friends and family join the procession of bringing the bride and groom to the groom's house.

The groom's house is decorated to receive the bride. The newly weds are welcomed into the household by a ceremony called the "Pani Varna".

The Process

- The newly weds are now standing in front of the door anxious to enter.

- The groom's mother performs the traditional aarti (puja) of the newly weds as they stand at the entrance of the house.

- She sprinkles some uncooked rice and flowers on both of then.

- She then performs the **"Pani Varna"** ceremony.

- She holds a garvi, also called a kalas or a pitcher (a small metal pot), half filled with water in her right hand.

- She takes the garvi and performs an aarti of the newly weds.

- On completion of one aarti, she tries to drink the water, but her son stops her from doing so.

- He stops her from drinking the water four times.

- She takes a sip of water after the fifth Pani Varna ceremony.

The significance of this ritual is that the mother is given the promise by the son that he remembers the four basic principles of leading a married life, which he took before getting ready for the sehra bandhi.

By stopping his mother from taking a sip of the water from the kalas, he says I will follow:

- "Dharm" – rightousness and religion and give my wife the honour and respect and lead a good life.

- The second time he says I will bring "Arth" I will earn and bring prosperity in the household.

- Third, I will follow "Kam" – when I have children, I will love them and my wife and I will be devoted parents.

- Fourth, "Moksh" – at the appropriate time in my life I will observe and perform my duties as you are doing today and seek detachment from worldly things and go in search of enlightenment in my life.

- Finally, I will bring honour to the family.

The mother now knows that her son is fully aware of his responsibilities and takes a sip of water and asks them both to enter the house. The water signifies purity of thought and action.

The groom then asks his bride to enter first, taking the first step with the right foot.

TAPPING THE KALAS

She enters the house and in the doorwary is a kalas filled with rice.

- She taps the kalas, filled with uncooked rice, so the rice spills over.

- She is entering the household of her in-laws, having left her parents house, where she threw the rice over her head.

- She wished prosperity for the household she has left behind and is now asking for prosperity for the house she is entering.

- Her husband follows her.

- They are both seated.

- They are fed sweets and given some refreshments.

- A cup of tea is a welcome sight at this time.

THINGS FOR THIS CEREMONY ARE:

1 Thali 6" with a jyot, some flowers, and some uncooked rice.	
1 Kalas, (garvi) with water in i	
1 Kalas (garvi) with uncooked rice in it	
Flower petals	
Uncooked rice	

Gana and Kangna Khalna

This ceremony relieves both the bride and the groom of all the accessories that they have been wearing since the start of the wedding.

- First of all the groom's mother takes off the kileray the bride has been wearing.

- The groom then unties the gana the bride has been wearing.

- The bride does the same, and unties the gana of the groom has been wearing.

This untying of the gana is a game play in order to relax the couple. The male and the female camps back their own clan on this occasion. The female camp is usually the winner. But there are always exceptions to the rule. The next game is Kangna Khalna.

The Process

- The bracelets "ganas" (the untied strings), a gold ring, and two silver coins are put in a large bowl of water and milk, Kachi Lasi (milk and water in equal quantities).

- Some flower petals are added to the bowl to disguise the five items that have been placed in kachi lasi.

- The bride and the groom sit opposite each other with this bowl in the middle.

- The couple do not have to sit on the floor; they can be seated in comfortable chairs for this ceremony.

- A family member conducts the proceedings.

- On the count of three, the five items are dropped in the mixture of kachi lasi.

- Both the bride and the groom try and search for the gold ring.

- Whosoever gets the gold ring first, wins the round.

- This game is played for the best of five rounds.

The male and female camps have lots of fun when this game is being played. Whosoever gets the gold ring three times, wins this game. Once again it is considered that the winner of the game will be wearing the pants in the household.

The ceremony is concluded when the games are over and with a final cup of tea the family say their farewells and leave.

*After this ceremony the wedding is **officially** over. As the family members depart the house of the wedded couple, they are given a remembrance gifts by the parents of the groom. These gifts are not mandatory. It is just a way of saying thank you for coming to the wedding and being part of our festivities.*

OPTIONAL CEREMONIES

ROKA

The Roka ceremony is conducted after the prospective bride and groom have met and given their consent to marry each other. The aim of this ceremony is that both these individuals will no longer be part of the eligible kingdom. Roka literally means, "stop". This ceremony is just an assurance to the families concerned that both the bride and groom are committed to each other. This ceremony is optional.

This ceremony is performed as soon as the couple have decided to take the plunge and it could be a year or 6-9 months in advance. It can be performed at any time and anywhere. Traditionally the ceremony is performed in the house of the bride or a venue selected by them.

The father of the bride or any other elder member of the family give their son-in-law to be some Indian sweets to eat and a small gift, which could be cash, or otherwise. He accepts these gifts and gets up and touches their feet and gets their blessings.

THINGS REQUIRED FOR THE CEREMONY ARE:

Cash or any other present that you wish to give to the son-in-law to be.	
Lunch, dinner and party are optional extras and dependant upon the families themselves.	

GHAR GHARDOLI

In the olden times, either the mother or the sister-in-law in the family went out to fetch water for the family. During the wedding of her brother-in-law, it was customary that the sister in law went out and fetched water for the groom to take a bath. In return the mother-in-law would give her daughter in law a present. Now-a-days, this is just a ritual for fun and frolics and is tagged along at the end of the sangeet or mehndi ceremony.

THINGS REQUIRED FOR THIS CEREMONY ARE

Gift for the daughter in law	

MOOH DIKHAI KI RASAM

In times gone by, all the family and friends could not join the marriage party, the "Baraat". Therefore, when the "Doli" arrived, the bride was introduced to the members of the family and friends.

This ceremony has no significance in the present day and age. Both the couple and their families are known to each other. This ceremony can be tagged along after the Khagana Kholna, if you really want to do it.

PHERA DALNA

This ceremony is the bride and the groom visiting the family of the bride after the wedding. It is a visit of reassurance for the bride's family that everything is ok and the bride is not feeling home sick. This ceremony was of important in the olden times when the couple did not know each other. In the present time, it is just time to catch up with the family after the couple return from their holidays, or having had a break from the activities of the wedding.

Puja of the Ancestors and Mata Durga

This is a very personal function and performed as a mark of respect for the departed souls in the family. This ritual in some families is optional.

The location of this ceremony is the groom's parental home and is performed mid morning, the day after the arrival of the doli.

The Process

- The groom's mother and father set up a small shrine of "Goddess Mata Durga".

- A small area is allocated, inviting the ancestors to come and attend the ceremony.

- Fresh food is prepared. The speciality is "halva", a sweet pudding made out of semolina.

- The immediate family members are invited to this ceremony.

- The prayers are said in the form of bhajans.

- The ceremony is concluded by singing the aarti.

- The newly weds take the front seat.

- One of the elders in the family generally performs this puja

- The newly weds are given the prasad, and thereafter all the family members are given prasad.

- The money that is collected during the puja ceremony is given to the unmarried girls in the family to share.

THINGS REQUIRED FOR THE CEREMONY ARE:

Temporary Shrine for Mata Durga	
Jyot, ghee and agarbati (incense sticks)	
Some dry fruit for Prasad	
Halva for Prasad	
Some money to offer the Goddess	
Food as per the wishes of the family	

RELIGIOUS SIGNIFICANCE
AND THE PROCESSES

GANPATHI VANDHANA AND DURGA PUJA

BACKGROUND

All Hindus perform Ganpathi Vandhana and Durga Puja before the commencement of any occasion. This may be a wedding ceremony, moving into a new house, the birth of a child, a child making its first visit to school. Most Hindus pay their respects to Ganpathi and Mata Durga before they leave their homes each morning and before they go to bed at night.

Ganpathi – the elephant Godhead is the son of Lord Shiva and Parvati, and is the remover of all obstacles and blesses us so that the activity we are going to undertake comes to a successful conclusion. Therefore, Ganpathi Vandhana is asking for his blessings before the commencement of any activity. This could be a simple prayer to Lord Ganesh on your own, or an elaborate one with family and friends, with the help of a professional pandit, Sometimes people do a simple Ganpathi Vandhanda at the commencement of each activity and have one grandeur prayer session on a special day.

This ceremony, Ganpathi and Maa Durga vandhana, in its most simple form is, standing in front of Lord Ganesh and Maa Durga and reciting their name and seeking their blessings. Touch the feet of Lord Ganesh and Maa Durga and the ceremony is concluded. Most of the elders in Indian homes are capable of doing this ceremony in its simple form. Listed below is detailed explanation of this prayer and its procedure. If the families want to go down this route, then a pandit is required, and the pandit takes the lead in these prayers.

The Process for the Puja

1. Make a temporary temple using a table. Cover the table and decorate it. Put photos, muritis of Gods in this shrine for example, Lord Krishn, Hanumanji, Lord Ram, Mata Durga, Lord Shiv and Parvati.

2. Take a murti of Lord Ganesh and put it in a thali. Lord Ganesh is bathed in Panch Amrit (Panch Amrit is a mixture of ghee, yoghurt, honey, milk and ganga jal) and then with water. This is done by pouring the panch amrit over the murti using a bowl. He is then washed off with water in the similar manner. Lord Ganesh is dried with a towel and placed in the shrine.

3. Similarly, take a murti of Mata Durga and bath it in Panch Amrit and then water. The Murti is dried and placed in the shrine.

4. First of all you put tilak, (a mark with the red powder, Kum Kum) on Lord Ganesh's forehead, using the third finger of your right hand.

5. Take some uncooked rice and put these on Lord Ganesh's forehead.

6. Lord Ganesh is then offered clothing in the form of a garland, using mauli (Indian red and white sacred thread).

7. You then sprinkle flower where Lord Ganesh is sitting to welcome him to your house.

8. A jyot is lit in the temple and this jyot is offered to the deities.

9. Some form of Prasad is placed in front of the deities. It could be methi, (Indian sweets) or as per the choice of the family concerned.

10. The same process from 4 to 9 is repeated for Mata Durga as well.

Kalas Puja

Kalas is a metal pot (Gardvi) which is placed in the middle of a temporary shrine. Kalas puja is prayers to the five elements namely, air, earth, fire, water and sky, the five Gods of the universe. We pray that the five elements always stay in situ. A coconut symbolizes a human being. The human being should be as strong as a coconut on the outside and as fair and compassionate as a coconut is in the inside.

The Puja

1. Half fill the Kalas with water.

2. Take five beetle nut leaves (or any other leaves, if beetle nut leaves are not available).

3. Place these leaves around the mouth of the Kalas.

4. Take the coconut. Put the sign of OM or Swastika on the face of the coconut, bushy side is the top side. (Follow the sketch above)

5. Place the coconut on the mouth of the Kalas in between the leaves.

6. Pick the Kalas up and put it in the middle of the temporary shrine. The Kalas is placed in the shrine by either the bride/ groom or their mother.

7. The Kalas is left standing in the shrine until the puja is over.

8. At the end of the puja, the coconut is picked up and broken. This signifies a breakaway from the negative influences in life and move towards a positive attitude in life. In other words we give up Kam, Krudh, Lobh, Moh and Ahnkar (attachment, greed, deceit, jealousy and anger) and become understanding, compassionate, respectful and trustworthy individuals.

9. The Kalas is gently rocked to inform the five Gods that the prayers are over.

10. The water in the Kalas is then sprinkled around the house and the rest is poured into the house plants.

The prayers start by singing the Ganpathi Vandhana followed by bhajans to Mata Durga and the other deities.

The above is a simplified, do it yourself version of the Puja. If a pandit is called upon to perform this puja, he will do an elongated version and guide you through various mantras.

MATA DURGA PUJA BACKGROUND

Most Hindu Punjabis perform Durga Puja as a special occasion. The Durga puja is preceded by Lord Ganesh's puja (The process is common to both 1-9 refers)

The Goddess Durga took her form to destroy demons that were making life difficult for the Devas All the Gods gave their powers to Maa Durga so that she would then be all-powerful and kill the demons, which could not be killed when the Gods tried to destroy them individually. She is the Universal Mother, who has taken a vow to protect us all. Therefore, we pray to Mata Durga, hoping that all our internal demons, the demons within us of jealousy, greed, anger, deceit and vengeance will be destroyed and we will become better human beings. We refer to her as "Ma" mother, because, mother is the first Guru as per "Shrimat Bhagwat Gita" – the first teacher and she guides her children as they go through the various stages of life.

This puja is performed a week or ten days before the wedding day and is usually under the guidance of a pandit who leads the family when they are doing the puja. Sometimes families do not call upon the services of a pandit and do it on their own with the help of the elders in the family.

This puja can be done at a venue or a local temple.

Durga Puja is of two kinds:

- Jagran – when it is performed through the night.

- Chaunki – when it is performed at any other time of the day for a short period.

When it is an all night affair, the puja is called "Mata Durga Jagran". "Jagran" means keeping awake through the night. The puja starts at 9.00pm and ends at 6.00am. When Durga Puja is performed any other time for about three hours, it is referred to as "Mata ki Chaunki". These prayers can be held in the afternoon or early evening.

There are no hard and fast rules about the timing of this puja and it is performed taking into account the time and convenience of the parties concerned. It has become a custom in the modern times to do this puja, but it is not mandatory.

THE PUJA

The Process of the Puja is same as above from 4 to 9.

Mata Durga is offered the garland and some additional items and these are:

THINGS REQUIRED FOR THIS PUJA ARE:

1. Some bangles	
2. Sindhoor	
3. Bindi	
4. Mehndi	
5. A red chunni or scarf	
6. A set of nine chunnis (or any other gifts) which will be handed over to nine young girls are placed in the shrine.	
7. Prasad items are a mixture of 5 kinds of dried fruit.	
8. An Indian sweet, called "halva"	
9. A savoury dish made with black chick peas.	

These additional items are placed in a thali and offered to the Goddess. The devotees sing devotional songs for a couple of hours.

THE CONCLUDING PRAYERS

All Hindu prayers end by singing an "Aarti". In the case of Maa Durga, before the conclusion, the bride/groom and their parents stand up and hold a coconut in their hands. This is their final offer to Maa Durga. This is called the 'Ardas'. They are seeking the blessings of the Universal Mother and they hope she will guide them all the way. The verses of the "Ardas" are listed below. Other members of the family and friends can also partake in the "Ardas", if they so wish. Each person can come forward and perform an "Ardas" for themselves. All other members who want to do Ardas, do not have to hold a coconut in their hands. They can offer her whatever they like.

The nine scarves (or other gifts), which have been kept in the shrine are then give to nine young girls. The significance of this ritual is that Maa Durga took nine different forms when she had to kill the demons.

The Maa Durga's Aarti is sung to conclude her Jagran or Chaunki. Some people prefer to sing both the Aartis. During the Aarti, the family rotate the jyot around the shrine.

All attendees take the blessings of the Lord by folding their hands over the Jyot (the Indian candle that was lit in front of deities). The prasad is first offered to the deities and then it is offered to all those who have attended the ceremony.

THINGS NEEDED FOR THIS CEREMONY ARE:
PUJA SAMAGRI (THINGS NEEDED FOR THE PRAYERS)

1 Steel glass (tumbler), 4 caulis (Bowls), 1 Kalas (Gardvi), 4 steel Thalis 8" diameter (plates) and 4 desert spoons	
Cotton wool	
Mauli – red thread 1 roll	
Ghee – clarified butter	
Kum Kum – red powder	
Agarbati – incense sticks	
Panch Amrit – mixture made up of milk, a drop of ghee (clarified butter), honey, Ganga jal and a bit of yoghurt – prepared in one of the 4 bowls.	
Uncooked rice – a bowl full	
Flowers and flower petal	
2 Coconuts (one for the Kalas and the other for the Aradas).	
5 Pan leaves, (Beetle nut leaves) or any other leaves.	
1 Red Chunni – scarf, 1 tube/put mehndi (henna), 6 bangles, 1 pkt bindi – Offerings to Goddess Durga	
Mixed fresh fruits	

Mixture of 5 dry fruits - almonds, cashew nuts, and pistachio nuts (unsalted), Raisins, dry apricots, walnuts, dry dates etc. (These can be varied, as you wish).	
Mixture of - elaichi (cardamoms), laving (cloves), Saunf and mishri (Indian sugar candy) – small quantity.	
Kale chancy (Black chickpeas) cooked. – Prasad	
Halva, (semolina based Indian homemade sweet) – Prasad	
Chunins/scarfs 8, representing the nine Goddesses, to be given to young girls (under the age of 10) at the end of the ceremony.	
Puja thali to put the jyot and incense stick on it	

THE UNIVERSAL AARTI

Om Jai Jagdish Harae, Swami Jai Jagdish Harae (Swami)
Bhagt janan kay sankat, kshan may dur karay
Om Jai Jagdish hare.

Jo dhyavay phal pavay, dukh vinshay man ka (Swami dukh
Sukh sampati ghar avay, kasht mitay tan ki
Om Jai Jagdish harae.

Mata pita tum mere, sharan gahun kis ki (Swami sharan)
Tum bin aur na dooja, aas karo mai jis ki
Om Jai Jagdish harae.

Tum puran parmatma, tum antaryami (Swami tum)
Par brahm parmayshvar, tum sab ki swami
Om Jai Jagdish harae.

Tum karoona kay sagar, tum palan karti (Swami tum)
Mai moorakh kal kami, kripa karoo bharta
Om Jai Jagdish harae.

Tum ho ek agochar, sab kay pran pati (Swami sab)
Kis vidi milun daya may, tum ko mai koomati
Om Jai Jagdish harae.

Deen bandhu dukh harta, tum rakshak mere (Swami tum)
Karuna hasta badhao, upnay sharan lagao, dwar khara may tere
Om Jai Jagdish harae.

Vishay vikar mitao, pap haro deva (Swami pap)
Shraddha bhagti badhao, santan ki seva
Om Jai Jagish Harae.

Om Jai Jagdish harae, swami Jai Jagdish harae
Bhagat jano ki sankat, kshn may dooray karay
Om Jai Jagdish harae.

General concept of the Aarti

Hail to Thee, O Lord of the universe, remover of sorrow and Master of all.

Salutations and prostrations unto Thee. O instant remover of troubles of the devotees.

Thou reward those who sing Thy glories and remove their sorrows.

With Thy Name, happiness and prosperity dawn, and pain disappears.

O Lord! Thou art my Mother, Father and only refuge.

O Indwellers of all beings, Thou art perfect, absolute, omnipresent, omnipotent and omniscient.

O Ocean of compassion! Thou art the protector of all.

O merciful Master! Help me, who am ignorant and full of lust.

O Life of all life! Thou art only one and still invisible.

O merciful God! Guide ignorant beings to thy divine knowledge.
Thou art the support of the weak, the remover of sorrow and pain.

O my Protector! Bless me with thy compassionate hand.

I surrender to Thee.

Relieve me of passion and suffering.

Bless me with ever-lasting and ever-increasing faith, divine love and spirit of service.

Ganpathi Vandhana

Sanskrit Starting Prayer

Vakratunda mahaa kaaya suryo koti sama prabha,
Nirvignam Kurume deva, sarva kaarye shu sarvadaa.

O Lord with a curved trunk and a mighty body, whose lustre equals thousands of suns, I pray to thee. O Lord, remove the obstacles from all the actions I perform.

Ganpathi Aarti

Jai Ganesh Jai Ganesh Jai Ganesh Deva
Mata Jaki Parvati pita Maha Deva

Ladoyan ka bhog lagat sant karay seva
Har charay phool charay aur charay meva
Jai Ganesh Jai Ganesh Jai Ganesh Deva
Mata jaki Parvati pita Maha Deva.

Ek dant daya vant char buja dhari
Mathay pay sindhoor sohay musay ki savari
Dookhiyo kay dukh harat, parm anand deva
Mata jakee Parvati pita Maha Deva

Deenan ki laag rakh shub sutvari,
Kamna ko puri karo jauo balihari
Hey Deva kripa karo kasht haro mera
Mata jaki Parvati pita Maha Deva

Jao bhi tera dhayn dharay gyan milay usko
Choar tujay aur bhala dhayoo mai kisko
Charano may upni mujay sharan dena data
Mata Jaki Parvati pita Maha Deva

Jai Ganesh Jai Ganesh Jai Ganesh Deva
Mata jaki Parvati pita Maha Deva

MATA DURGA'S AARTI

Om Jai Ambay Gauri, Mata Jai Ambay Gauri,
Tum koo nish din dhayvat, har brahma shavri, Om Jai Ambay

Mang sindhoor virajat, teeko mrigmad ko,
Ujval sai duo naina, Chandra badan ni ko, Om Jai Ambay

Kanak saman kalavar, raktambar rajay,
Rakat pushp gal mala, kanthan par sajay, Om Jai Ambay

Kahar vahan rajat, kharak khapar dhati,
Sur nar munee jan savat, tin kay dukh hari, Om Jai Ambay

Kannan kundal shobhit, nasa gray moti,
Koti ka Chandra divakar, samrajat jyoti, Om Jai Ambay

Shub aashub vidharay, mahisah sur dhati,
Dhruv veelochan naina, nis din mad mati, Om Jai Ambay

Chausath yonyiya gaavat, nritya karat bharoo,
Bajat taal mridanga, aur bajat damroo, Om Jai Ambay

Bhuja char ati shobhit, kharka kapar dhari,
Man vanchit fal pavat, savat narnari, Om Jai Ambay

Kanchan thal virajat, ajar kapur bhati,
Shri maal katu may rajat, koti rattan jyoti, Om Jai Ambay

Shri Ambay ji ki aarti, jo koye jan gavay,
Kahat shivanand swami, sukh sampati pavay, Om Jai Ambay

Concluding Prayers

Sarve bhavantu sukhinah,
Sarve santu niramayah
Sarve bhadrani pashyantu
Ma kaschit dukh mapnuyat

O Lord! In Thee may all be happy. May all be free from misery, may all realise goodness, and may no one suffer pain.

Shanti Path (Hymn of Peace)

Om Dyauh santi rantariksham, shantih prithivi, shanty rapah, shanti roshadhayah shanti, Vanaspatayah shantir vishwedevah, shantir brahma, shantih sarvam shantih shantireva, shantih sah mah shantiredhi.
Om Shantih, Shantih, Shanti

There is peace in the heavenly region; there is peace in the atmosphere; peace reigns on the earth; the water is cooling; the herbs are healing; the plants are peace-giving; there is harmony in the celestial objects and perfection in knowledge; everything in the universe is peace; peace pervades everywhere. May that peace come to us all!

Aardas

Tere daas di "ardas" Maa tere shub charnay day paas,
Sweekar karee, barh paar kari, hath joor kharay,
Maa araz karay, sano galay nal laga, Maa charnay cha bitha,
Saday man vich upni jyoti jaga, Saday man vich upni jyoti jag, Yeh hai mere ardas, Yeh hai mere ardas.

Oh Mother we are standing before you, with folded hands, please accept our prayers and bestow your blessings on us. Lead us from darkness into enlightenment. Make us humble and devoted individuals.

OFFERING OF PRASAD TO THE DEITIES

Yeh bhojan chakyo hari, yeh Amrit hoojay,
Amrit Bhojan khayaki, tera Daas sharan ho jayay

Yeh Bhojan chakyo hari, yeh Amrit hoojay,
Amrit bhojan khayaki, tera Daas Amar ho jayay.

Boloo Bankiji Bihari Gansham Ki Jai
Boloo Sham Moorari Girwardhari Banwari Ki Jai
Boloo Bankiji Bhihari Nandlal Ki Jai
Nandlal Ki Jai, Nandlal Ki Jai

Please Lord accept our offerings. When you eat this food that we have placed before you, it will turn into "Amrit" a blessing for us. When we eat this food we will become devoted to you and follow the path of being peace loving individuals. We will become compassionate and do good deeds in life.

Salutations to the Lord, Salutations to the Lord.

Glossary

AGARBATI – INCENSE STICKS

AMRIT – mixture of five food ingredients, milk,
    honey, yoghurt, ghee and gangajal.

AMAR – Get enlightened and liberated

ARDAS – Seeking blessing of Maa Durga

AARTI – concluding salutations to the Lord

BHAGRA – Punjabi folk dance

BHARAT – the groom's wedding procession

CHAUNKI PUJA – Durga Puja held for a period of 2 to 3 hours

CHUNNI – an Indian name for a long scarf

CHURA – Red bangles which the bride wears

DEITY- the idol or photo of the Hindu Gods and Goddesses

DHOL – Punjabi percussion instrument

DHOOP – incense sticks

DOLI – a palanquin used for carrying females in the olden times.

DWAR PUJA – welcome of the Groom for the wedding ceremony

ELAICHI - cadimoms(CADIMOMS)

GANA – a string with 5 items beaded into it representing
    the five elements of the universe.

GATH BANDHAN – tying of the knot between the bride and groom.

GHEE – clarified butter

GHORI – means of transport for taking the groom to the marriage venue.

HALVA – semolina based indian homemade sweet.

HAVAN – ceremony of prayer using fire as its basis.

JYOT – an indian candle made with cotton wool, dipped in ghee.

GANGAJAL – holy water of the river Ganges

KALAS – a metal pot

KALE CHANCY – black chickpeas

KALECHARIS – rings made of gold or silver
given in settlement of shoe grabbing.

KAPOOR – camphor

KILERAY – umbrella shaped ornaments tied to
the iron bangle in front of the chura.

KUM KUM – red powder

LAJA - puffed rice

LAJAHOM – ceremony using puffed rice

LANGA – long skirt, worn as part of the wedding outfit

LAVING - cloves

LORD GANESH - Elephant Godhead

LORD SHIVA – father of Lord Ganesh

MANDAP – A four pillar canopy

MAMAS – brothers of a married sister (brother-in-law)

MAMI – wife of the brother of a married sister (Sister-in-law)

MANGAL FERE – going around the sacred fire

MANGALSUTRA – a black beaded sacred necklace

MANTRAS – Sanskrit verses of religious significance

MATA DURGA – Lord Shiva's wife, when she took a form to kill the demons.

MAULI – a roll of sacred red and white thread.

MEHNDI - henna

METHAI – Indian sweets

MILNI – meeting of two individuals

MISHRI - Indian sugar candy

PAGRI – a head gear

PANCH AMRIT – same as amrit made up of five ingredients

PANDITJI/Pujariji – a professional person who is conversant with Hindu Scriptures

PARVATI – Mother of Lord Ganesh and another name for Maa Durga

PRASAD – food offering to the deities.

PUJA – a prayer of devotion

SAMAGRI – mixture of ingredients offered to the fire when performing a havan

SANGEET – singing session

SAPTAPADI – seven vows

SARBALA – the best man

SAUNF - fennel

SHRINE – a place where deities are placed

SINDOOR – a red sacred powder, which is put in the head parting

SUHAG – a song sung to bless the bride for the commencement of her new life

SURMA – black mixture called kaajal

THALI - a steel plate

VAG FARAI – a gift given to the sisters after they tie vag to the ghori/car, in which the groom travels.

VARMALA - welcome garlands of the bride and the groom

VIDAI - departure of the bride from her home

WATNA - a paste made of flour, turmeric and oil

For further information or questions please contact:
kavita.kapoor@consultant.com

About the Author

I am of Indian origin, born in Nairobi, Kenya, the Daughter of Sri Ram Dass "Dass" Sunak and Shrimati Suhag Rani Sunak. It is from my parents, to whom this book is dedicated, that I learnt and began to love the cultural and religious aspects of Hinduism. My father was a prominent member of the Hindu Temple, both in Nairobi and Southampton. He was also a well-known poet and playwright. His and my mum's blessings have enabled me to achieve this milestone.

I am involved with my local community. In my spare time I try and increase awareness of Hinduism by holding exhibitions and giving talks at schools and colleges on the cultural aspects of our religion.

I have always been amazed at the conflicting information, advice, superstitions and reliance on ubiquitous aunties to guide us, when we are in the process of performing the most important ceremony of our lives.

I hope that some of the myths surrounding Hindu Wedding Ceremonies will be alleviated by referring to this book which has taken me over 3 years to complete.

Printed in the United Kingdom
by Lightning Source UK Ltd.
134317UK00001B/33-40/A